More Words
I Use
When I
Write

by
Alana Trisler
Patrice Howe Cardiel

Modern Learning Press is an imprint of School Specialty, Inc.

ISBN 978-0-8388-6070-0
Printed in Benton Harbor, MI, in July 2016

17 18 19 20 21 PPG 20 19 18 17 16

To all young writers and readers

A.T. and P.H.C.

Aa Aa

aardvark
ability
aboard
accept
accident
account

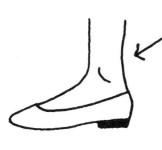

acorn
action
actor
adult
adventure
aeronautical
agreement

album
alligator
allowance
ambush
America
anesthetic
anger
ankle
ant
antelope
antenna
apartment
ape
apple
aquarium
argue
armadillo
army
artist
asleep

assignment
athlete
atmosphere
attack
attention
audience
auditorium
aunt
autograph
automatic
automobile
awake
away
awful
awkward

Aa Aa

Aa Aa

Aa Aa

_____ _____
_____ _____
_____ _____
_____ _____
_____ _____
_____ _____
_____ _____
_____ _____
_____ _____
_____ _____
_____ _____
_____ _____
_____ _____
_____ _____
_____ _____
_____ _____
_____ _____

Bb Bb

baboon
backstage
backward
balance
ballet
banana
bank
bargain
barn
basement
basketball
battlefield
bay
bazaar
bead
beam
beautiful
beaver
behave

beneath
beside
betray
bewitched
beyond
blanket
blister
blizzard
bloom

blossom
blush
bobcat
body
bodyguard
boom

born
bottle
boulder
bridge
bridle
brilliant
broken
brother
brute
bubble
bucket
buffalo
build
bulb
bundle
burn
bush
business
butter
button

B b   *Bb*

B b *Bb*

Bb   Bb

Cc Cc

cafeteria
calendar
camera
candle
canoe
canyon
captain
caption
capture
career
carnival
cartoon
cash
castle
ceiling
celebrate
cemetery
cent
cereal
challenge
character
chart

chase
chest
chew
child
chore
citizen
city
closet
cobra
collapse
collect
colony
communicate
community
computer
confuse

contest
continue
contract
control
copy
correct
courage
cousin
coward
coyote
cracker
crater
crayon
create
creature
crocodile
cupboard
curious
custodian
custom
customer

Cc Cc

Cc   Cc

D d *Dd*

dancer	detective	double
danger	dew	doughnut
dark	diagram	dove
dawn	different	down
deal	difficult	downtown
decide	dime	dragon
decoration	dinosaur	dream
deer	direction	dress
defeat	disappear	drink
delicate	disappoint	drive
delicious	discover	drop
delight	discovery	dungeon
deliver	discuss	during
demand	disturb	duty
department	dive	
describe	diver	
dessert	divide	
detail	dolphin	

Dd *Dd*

_____   _____

_____   _____

_____   _____

_____   _____

_____   _____

_____   _____

_____   _____

_____   _____

_____   _____

_____   _____

_____   _____

_____   _____

_____   _____

_____   _____

_____   _____

_____   _____

_____   _____

Dd *Dd*

Dd *Dd*

E e 𝓔 𝓮

eager
earth
east
eat
ecology
eel
effect
egg
either
eject
elbow
election
electricity
electronic
elephant
elevator
elf
eliminate
elk
embrace
emperor

empty
emu
enchanted
endangered
endurance
enemy
energy
engine
enormous
enough
enter
envelope
environment
equal
equipment

erase
escalator
escape
especially
evergreen
evidence
excite
exclaim
exhausted
expand
expect
expensive
experience
experiment
expert
explain
explore
express
extra
eyes

E e $\mathcal{E}$ e

Ee Ee

Ee Ee

F f $\mathcal{F}f$

fairy
fake
falcon
fan
fancy
fantastic
farewell
fate
father
faucet
favorite
fawn
feast
feather
female
ferret
fetch
fever
fib
field
fierce

fight
figure
film
finally
fingerprint
fisherman
flagpole
flamingo
flashlight
flavor
flight
float
flock
flood
flower
fold
foolish
forecast
foreign
forest
former

forward
fossil
fox
frail

freight
frog
frontier
frost
frown
fruit
funny
fur
furniture

F f *Ff*

F f *Ff*

F f *Ff*

Gg Gg

gallery
gallop
garden
gather
gaze
gentle
ghost
giant
gift
ginger
giraffe
glacier
glance
gland
glimpse
glitter
globe

glow
gnaw
gnu
goat
gopher
gorilla
grab
grandmother
grant
graph
grateful
grave
gravity
great
greedy
greet
grieve

grind
groceries
gross
guard
guess
guest
guide
guinea pig
guitar
gull

Gg   *Gg*

Hh *Hh*

habit · heel ·
habitat · helmet ·
hammer · helpful ·
hamster · herd ·
handicap · hero ·
handkerchief · hibernate ·
handsome · hippopotamus ·
handy · holler · hose
hard · hollow · hospital
hare · honest · humble
harness · honey · hummingbird
harvest · honor · humor
hate · hood · hundred
hawk · hoof · hunt
head · hook · hunter
headquarters · hope · hurricane
heart · horizon · hush
hearth · horrified · hydrant
heave · horror · hyena
hedgehog · horse

Hh   Hh

Hh *Hh*

Hh *Hh*

I i *Ii*

ibex
iceberg
icicle
idea
igloo
iguana
illustrate
image
imagination
impala

important
improve

information
initial

ink
inning
instant
instinct
instruct
instrument
interest
interview
invade
invent

I i   *Ii*

J j *J j*

jack-o-lantern	jellyfish	jockey
jackal	jet	join
jacket	jewel	joke
jackknife	jewelry	journey
jackrabbit	jingle	judge
jade		juggle
jaguar		juice
jail		jump
jealous		junk
jeep		jury

_____   _____

_____   _____

_____   _____

_____   _____

_____   _____

J j *Jj*

K k *K k*

kaleidoscope
kangaroo

katydid
kayak
keep

kept
kerosene
key
keyboard
kick
kid
kind
kingdom
kiss
kit
kitchen

kite
knapsack
knead
kneel
knife
knight
knock
knoll
knot
knowledge
koala

K k *Kk*

Ll   *Ll*

laboratory
ladder
ladybug
language
lava
lazy
leader
learn
least
leather
leave
legend
length

leopard
less
lettuce
level
library
life
light
lighthouse
lightning
lip
listen
lit
llama

lobster
lodge
loud
loudspeaker
lunch
luxury
lynx

_____
_____
_____
_____
_____

_____
_____
_____
_____
_____

Ll   *Ll*

Mm Mm

mad
magician
magnet
mole
mammoth
manage
manners
maple
marathon
mare
market
mat
mate
mayor
meadow
measure
mechanical
medal

medicine
meet
member
menagerie
menu
message
metal
meteor
microphone
microscope
million
minute
miracle
miss
mist
mistletoe
mixture
monkey

month
moose
motion
motor
mountain
mouse

munch
muscle
museum
mutt

M m 𝓜 𝓂

Mm *Mm*

Mm Mm

Nn *Nn*

napkin
national
naturalist
navigation
near
necklace
needle
neighbor
neighborhood
neither
nervous
newspaper

next
nibble
nickel

nickname
night
nine

noise
nonsense
north
notice
novel
nudge
nugget
numeral
nurse
nutrition

Nn 𝓝𝓃

Oo Oo

oasis
obey
object
observe
obvious
ocean
octopus
offer
office
official
olympics
opera
operate

operation
opinion
opossum
opposite
orangutan
orchestra

order
ordinary
oriental
original
ornament
ostrich
otter
out
outlet
overcome
overnight
owe

_____
_____
_____
_____

_____
_____
_____
_____

Oo Oo

_____   _____
_____   _____
_____   _____
_____   _____
_____   _____
_____   _____
_____   _____
_____   _____
_____   _____
_____   _____
_____   _____
_____   _____
_____   _____
_____   _____
_____   _____
_____   _____
_____   _____

Pp Pp

packet
page
palace
panda
parachute
pass
passenger
path
patient
pattern
pause
peacock
pebble
penguin
perfect
perform
permanent
pester
petition
photograph
phrase

picnic
pipe
plain

plane
planet
planetarium
plant
plot
poem
poet
poetry
poison
police
pond
porcupine

potato
powder
practice
prairie
predict
prefer
prepare
pretend
prevent
prey
principal
probably
profession
professor
progress
project
promise
protect
proud
puppet
python

P p   P p

P p P p

Pp   Pp

Qq 2q

quail
quarter
queen
quest
question
quick

quiet
quilt
quit
quiver
quiz

Qq 2q

Rr Rr

raccoon
radar
raft
raisin
rapids
rattlesnake
realize
recall
receive
recipe
reckless
recognize
record
refrigerator
regular
reindeer
release
relief
remark
remember

remove
repair
repeat
replace
report
rescue
reservation
resist
respect
responsibility
restaurant
return
reward
rhyme
rhythm
rifle
ring
rise
risk
robe

robot

roof
rough
route
rowboat
royal
rubber
rule
ruler
rumble
run
rusty

Rr Rr

_____   _____

_____   _____

_____   _____

_____   _____

_____   _____

_____   _____

_____   _____

_____   _____

_____   _____

_____   _____

_____   _____

_____   _____

_____   _____

_____   _____

_____   _____

_____   _____

Rr Rr

Rr Rr

Ss *Ss*

safe
salt
sandwich
satisfy
scent
science
scientist
scissors
scratch
season
selfish
sense
sentence
serious
servant
serve
several
shake
shape
share
shark

sheep
shoulder
shrink
shuttle
shy

sick
sift
signal
skeleton
sketch
skyscraper
sleepy
slime
soft
south

spank
speech
spell
spider
sponge
squeeze
staple
stare
steal
stomach
strength
struggle
studio
subject
substitute
sugar
suggest
swallow
swamp
sympathy
symphony

Ss   *Ss*

Ss   *Ss*

Ss   *Ss*

Tt Tt

tadpole
tale
tarantula
target
taxi
tease
teeth
telegraph
telephone
tent

tepee
terrain
terrible
terrific
terrify

test
theater
thermometer
thief
thread
threaten
tide
tight
timid
tiptoe
tissue
toad
tomato
tongue
tonight
tonsils
tornado
tortoise
total
tough
tour
towel

tradition
trail
trample
trap
trapeze
treasure
treat
tremendous
triangle
tribe
trip
trouble
trunk
truth
tube
tumble
tunnel
turtle
twinkle
twister

Tt *Tt*

T t   *T t*

T t   *Tt*

Uu Uu

ugly	uniform	upon
umbrella	unique	upper
uncover	universe	upward
under	university	urge
understand	unusual	urgent
unfinished	unwrap	useful
unhappy		useless
unicorn		usher

Uu Vu

V v $\mathcal{V}\nu$

vacant	vanish	vicious
vacation	vase	victim
vaccine	vast	video
vacuum	vegetable	view
vague	vehicle	village
valentine	venom	villain
valuable	veranda	violin
value	verdict	visible
vampire	vest	vitamin
van	veterinarian	vocabulary
		voice
		volcano
		volunteer
		vote
		vulture

V v $\mathcal{U}u$

Ww Ww

waffle
wag
wagon
walrus
waltz
wander

war
warm
warning
wary
wash
wasp
watermelon
waterproof
wave
weak
weary
weasel

weather
weave
weird
welcome
west
whale
which
whimper
whistle
whitecap
wicked
wide

widow
wigwam
windmill
wing
wipe
wisdom
witch
wobble
wolf
won
wonder
wonderful
woodchuck
wound
wow
wrap
wreath
wrestle

Ww   *Ww*

Ww   Ww

X x *Xx*

x-ray
xerox
xylophone

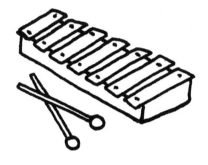

_____   _____

_____   _____

_____   _____

_____   _____

X x 𝒳 𝓍

Yy Yy

yank
yard
yarn
yawn
year
yes
yield
yogurt
you
young
your
youth
yummy

Y y   *Y* *y*

Z z *Zz*

zap	zigzag	zone
zebra	zip	zoo
zero	zipper	zoom

Z z   *Zz*

DAYS OF THE WEEK

Sunday	Sun.
Monday	Mon.
Tuesday	Tues.
Wednesday	Wed.
Thursday	Thurs.
Friday	Fri.
Saturday	Sat.

MONTHS OF THE YEAR

January	Jan.
February	Feb.
March	Mar.
April	Apr.
May	
June	
July	
August	Aug.
September	Sept.
October	Oct.
November	Nov.
December	Dec.

CONTRACTIONS

aren't	are not
can't	cannot
couldn't	could not
didn't	did not
doesn't	does not
don't	do not
hasn't	has not
haven't	have not
I'll	I will
I'm	I am
isn't	is not
it's	it is
I've	I have
let's	let us
shouldn't	should not
they'll	they will
wasn't	was not
we'll	we will
we're	we are
won't	will not
wouldn't	would not
you'll	you will
you're	you are

THE FIFTY STATES

Alabama	Louisiana	Ohio
Alaska	Maine	Oklahoma
Arizona	Maryland	Oregon
Arkansas	Massachusetts	Pennsylvania
California	Michigan	Rhode Island
Colorado	Minnesota	South Carolina
Connecticut	Mississippi	South Dakota
Delaware	Missouri	Tennessee
Florida	Montana	Texas
Georgia	Nebraska	Utah
Hawaii	Nevada	Vermont
Idaho	New Hampshire	Virginia
Illinois	New Jersey	Washington
Indiana	New Mexico	West Virginia
Iowa	New York	Wisconsin
Kansas	North Carolina	Wyoming
Kentucky	North Dakota	

CLASSMATES AND FRIENDS

_____   _____

_____   _____

_____   _____

_____   _____

_____   _____

_____   _____

_____   _____

_____   _____

_____   _____

_____   _____

_____   _____

_____   _____

_____   _____

_____   _____

_____   _____

_____   _____

_____   _____

FAMILY

_____   _____

_____   _____

_____   _____

_____   _____

_____   _____

_____   _____

_____   _____

_____   _____

_____   _____

_____   _____

_____   _____

_____   _____

_____   _____

_____   _____

_____   _____

_____   _____

NUMBERS	ORDINALS
one	first
two	second
three	third
four	fourth
five	fifth
six	sixth
seven	seventh
eight	eighth
nine	ninth
ten	tenth
eleven	eleventh
twelve	twelfth
thirteen	thirteenth
fourteen	fourteenth
fifteen	fifteenth
sixteen	sixteenth
seventeen	seventeenth
eighteen	eighteenth
nineteen	nineteenth
twenty	twentieth